▶ ESSENTIAL SURVIVAL STORIES

ROCK AND MOUNTAIN SURVIVAL STORIES

BY LIZ SONNEBORN

Essential Library
An Imprint of Abdo Publishing
abdobooks.com

ABDOBOOKS.COM

Published by Abdo Publishing, a division of ABDO, PO Box 398166, Minneapolis, Minnesota 55439. Copyright © 2024 by Abdo Consulting Group, Inc. International copyrights reserved in all countries. No part of this book may be reproduced in any form without written permission from the publisher. Essential Library™ is a trademark and logo of Abdo Publishing.

Printed in the United States of America, North Mankato, Minnesota.
102023
012024

THIS BOOK CONTAINS RECYCLED MATERIALS

Cover Photo: Shutterstock Images
Interior Photos: Shutterstock Images, 1, 4–5, 43, 52–53, 56, 58; Red Line Editorial, 7; Bettmann/Getty Images, 8; Amanda Mohler/Shutterstock Images, 14–15; Daniel Prudek/Shutterstock Images, 16; James Marvin Phelps/Shutterstock Images, 19; Saulius Damulevicius/Shutterstock Images, 22; Everett Collection Historical/Alamy, 26; Lysogor Roman/Shutterstock Images, 29; Evening Standard/Hulton Archive/Getty Images, 33, 44; Martin Bernetti/AFP/Getty Images, 35; Vasiq Eqbal/Shutterstock Images, 38–39; AP Images, 51; Ondra Vacek/Shutterstock Images, 62; Ian Cook/The Chronicle Collection/Getty Images, 65; Danita Delimont/Shutterstock Images, 66–67; E. Pablo Kosmicki/AP Images, 70; Beth Wald/Aurora Photos/Cavan Images/Alamy, 73; FlixPix/Searchlight Pictures/Alamy, 75; Ross D. Franklin/AP Images, 77; Evan Agostini/AP Images, 79; Denis Tangney Jr./iStockphoto, 80–81; Isaac Shiffman/iStockphoto, 84; Emily Russo Miller/Juneau Empire/AP Images, 89; Charles Sykes/Invision/AP Images, 90; William Perugini/Shutterstock Images, 92–93; Galyna Andrushko/Shutterstock Images, 96

Editor: Marie Pearson
Series Designer: Maggie Villaume

Library of Congress Control Number: 2023939428

PUBLISHER'S CATALOGING-IN-PUBLICATION DATA
Names: Sonneborn, Liz, author.
Title: Rock and mountain survival stories / by Liz Sonneborn
Description: Minneapolis, Minnesota: Abdo Publishing, 2024 | Series: Essential survival stories | Includes online resources and index.
Identifiers: ISBN 9781098292232 (lib. bdg.) | ISBN 9798384910176 (ebook)
Subjects: LCSH: Survival--Juvenile literature. | Adventure and adventurers--Juvenile literature. | Mountaineering accidents--Juvenile literature. | Mountaineering--Search and rescue operations--Juvenile literature. | Wilderness survival--Juvenile literature.
Classification: DDC 613.69--dc23

CONTENTS

CHAPTER ONE
STRANDED IN THE ANDES 4

CHAPTER TWO
THE DANGERS OF ROCKS AND MOUNTAINS 14

CHAPTER THREE
OVER THE MOUNTAIN 26

CHAPTER FOUR
DESCENDING THE OGRE 38

CHAPTER FIVE
THE END OF THE ROPE 52

CHAPTER SIX
TRAPPED BY A BOULDER 66

CHAPTER SEVEN
SAVING JOHN 80

CHAPTER EIGHT
SURVIVING ROCKS AND MOUNTAINS 92

ESSENTIAL FACTS 100
GLOSSARY 102
ADDITIONAL RESOURCES 104
SOURCE NOTES 106
INDEX 110
ABOUT THE AUTHOR 112

The accounts in Chapters One, Five, Six, and Seven mention thoughts of suicide.

CHAPTER 1

STRANDED IN THE ANDES

The members of Uruguay's national championship rugby team from the Old Christians Club were boarding a small chartered plane at the airport in Mendoza, Argentina, on the afternoon of October 13, 1972. They were pumped about this final leg in their journey. They were headed for Santiago, Chile, to play an exhibition game. The plane had a flight crew of five. Most of the other 40 passengers were friends and family of the team members, eager to cheer them on.[1]

Aside from the game, the players were also looking forward to the trip itself. The team members, ranging in age from 18 to 26, were up for an adventure in a different country. The flight itself even promised

◀ The Andes run across South America from the Caribbean to the southern tip of the continent.

a new experience. Having grown up along Uruguay's coast, they were thrilled about the view of the Andes Mountains they would have from the plane's windows. It would be their first glimpse of snow.

THE CRASH

On the flight, the players were tossing around rugby balls when the plane hit a patch of turbulence. Passengers were joking. Some of the players began to run from one side of the plane to the other to see if they could make the airplane rock back and forth.

The mood shifted when the passengers saw they were approaching a wall of rock. The pilot screamed, "Power! More power!" as the engines roared and the entire plane began to shake.[2] Then, to everyone's horror, the airplane sideswiped a mountain. The wings and the tail were ripped off. Five passengers

OFF COURSE

The cause of the crash of the Uruguayan plane was a simple matter of pilot error. The pilots were flying a Fairchild FH-227, a twin-engine airplane owned by the Uruguayan Air Force. Because the plane was not built to fly higher than 22,500 feet (6,860 m), they charted a course through a low pass in the Andes.[3] An hour after takeoff, the crew told air traffic controllers that they were flying over the pass, but they were mistaken. As they lowered the plane to prepare for landing, they were in fact still in the Andes, a miscalculation that ended in disaster.

▲ The plane carrying the Uruguayan rugby team crashed in Argentina's Andes near San Fernando, Chile. The pilot had intended to take the plane through a pass in the mountains south of Santiago, turning north once the plane had cleared the pass.

and two crew members were sucked out of the giant hole in the rear of the plane. The fuselage, carrying the remaining passengers and crew, landed in a snow-covered valley, sliding on the ground like a giant sled for 3,000 feet (910 m) before finally coming to a stop near the Chilean border.[4]

Shocked and terrified, the survivors began to emerge, crawling over the bodies of the dead. Many of the seats had broken loose, crushing passengers as the plane made its crash landing. The pilot, pinned in the cockpit, was near death. He begged two boys to find the gun he had in his bag so he could kill himself. The boys refused because they thought suicide was immoral. The pilot soon died of his injuries.

STAYING ALIVE

Miraculously, 29 out of the 45 people on the plane were alive. Some were severely injured. Others escaped with barely a scratch. Passenger Roberto Canessa was one of the lucky ones. As he surveyed the situation, he thought, "In a few hours, they'll come looking for me. I've escaped. I've made it. I'm alive. Lucky for me, it's all over."[5]

As they waited to be rescued, the survivors worked to stay alive. They spent nights in the fuselage, using seat covers as blankets to protect themselves from the bitterly cold temperatures outside. They warmed snow on pieces of

▼ Stuck on a snowy mountain, there was little food nearby for the survivors to gather.

metal from the plane placed in the sunlight to make drinking water. Marcelo Pérez, the rugby team's captain, took control of their tiny food supply, doling out equal-sized squares of chocolate to each person each day. The team's doctor had been killed in the crash, so medical students like Canessa did what they could to help the injured.

The third day on the mountain, Nando Parrado, who had been knocked unconscious in the crash, finally opened his eyes. The last thing he remembered was sitting on the plane with his mother and sister. As his teammates told him what happened, Parrado asked, "Where's Mom? Where's Susy?"[6] They explained his mother was dead and his sister was injured. A few days later, Susy died in her brother's arms.

Throughout the ordeal, the survivors struggled to stay hopeful that help was on the way. They had a transistor radio, so they could listen to news reports of the rescue mission that was underway.

> "Discipline, teamwork, endurance. We worked as a team, a rugby team, there was never a fight. Condemned to die without any hope, we transported the rugby feeling to the cold fuselage at 12,000 feet [3,660 m]."[7]
>
> —Nando Parrado on the survivors' sense of solidarity, 2015

A FAILED RESCUE

Several factors contributed to the failure of the rescue mission. One was that the fuselage of the airplane was white. Visually, it blended into the mountain snow, making it nearly impossible to see from the air. It would have been most visible at midday, but because of turbulent air currents, the mission was suspended during that time. The crew of the plane also had incorrectly reported their location to air traffic controllers, so the rescue mission began its search in the wrong place.

Periodically, airplanes flew overhead. Each time, they were sure they had been spotted, only to be disappointed when no rescuers arrived.

A GRIM DECISION

After several days, the survivors could not help feeling they were doomed. As their food supplies dwindled, they were so weak they could barely move. The young rugby players began to whisper among themselves about what now seemed the only way to stay alive, though no one wanted to be the first to say it out loud. Eduardo Strauch remembered feeling relieved when his cousin Adolfo came out and said, "Either we do it or we die."[8]

The survivors decided to hold a meeting in the fuselage to discuss what they had been afraid to talk about—eating the bodies of their dead friends and loved ones. As Roman Catholics, they saw cannibalism as a deep violation of their religious views. But some survivors argued that their duty to return to their families was far more important than any religious or cultural taboo.

Pérez worked to persuade those who were still hesitant. One survivor recalled how at the Last Supper, shortly before Jesus's death, Jesus told his disciples that the bread they were eating was his body and the wine they were drinking was his blood. This biblical story is commemorated in Catholic Mass as Communion. During this ritual, priests offer congregants a wafer and a sip of wine, which Catholics believe transform into the body and blood of Jesus.

Placing their forced cannibalism within this familiar religious framework, some survivors were convinced that the act was not morally wrong. Once most decided they had no choice but to eat meat from the bodies, they made a pact. They all gave their fellow survivors permission to consume their bodies if they should die next.

Trying to treat the bodies with as much respect as possible, the survivors began eating daily rations of the remains. After making the decision to do so, they rarely thought about their cannibalism. As survivor Gustavo Zerbino later said, "The taboo is mental. Once you break it, it's like anything else. You get used to it."[9] The decision also made many see their new lives on the mountain as completely foreign from the world they used to know.

ON THEIR OWN

On their tenth day on the mountain, Pérez, Parrado, and a few other men set up an antenna to get the latest news on the radio. They tuned in at the end of a dispiriting news report. It explained that the Chilean Air Rescue Services had ended the search for their plane because at that point, rescuers believed that no one could possibly have survived the crash.

    Devastated by the news, Pérez and several others began to weep, while Parrado, stone-faced, lifted his eyes to the mountains that imprisoned them. A teammate named Gustavo Nicolich came out of the fuselage, saw their faces, and immediately guessed what they had heard on the radio.

    Nicolich asked Pérez what they should tell the other survivors. Pérez insisted they say nothing. If the others knew, they would give up all hope. Nicolich replied, "No. We must tell them. They must know the worst."[10]

    Nicolich climbed into the fuselage and yelled out, "Hey, boys, there's some good news! We just heard it on the radio. They've called off the search." After a stunned silence, one of the men asked how that was possibly good news. Nicolich responded, "Because it means that we're going to get out of here on our own."[11]

How the Uruguayan rugby team did that is one of the best-known and most dramatic survival stories ever. Over decades, it has been recounted in numerous books and movies. But it is only one of many amazing tales of survival in mountainous and rocky terrains. These inspiring stories celebrate some of the most admirable traits people can have, including courage, resourcefulness, resilience, and self-sacrifice. But driving them all is perhaps the most human of all impulses —the desire to live, even when faced with what appears to be certain death.

A VISION OF SURVIVORS

Many of the parents of the rugby players were furious when the Chilean government ended its search for survivors only eight days after the crash. In desperation, one mother contacted Gerard Croiset, a Dutch clairvoyant, asking him if he could give her evidence that her son was still alive. Croiset said he had a vision that the plane had crashed in a mountain valley. He could see the pilots were dead, but there were other survivors. Although some parents were skeptical, others were convinced by Croiset's vision that their sons had survived.

CHAPTER 2

THE DANGERS OF ROCKS AND MOUNTAINS

Anyone who has ever gazed up at a majestic peak or down into a deep canyon knows that mountainous and rocky terrains are among the world's most beautiful natural wonders. Vacationers and adventurers travel great distances to view marvels such as Mount Everest or the Grand Canyon. But mountainous and rocky areas also pose many dangers, particularly when people underestimate their vulnerability in these wild spaces.

There is no formal definition for what distinguishes a mountain from a hill. But generally mountains are landforms that reach a high elevation, have steep

◀ Mountains and canyons, such as the Grand Canyon, attract visitors for many reasons, including to admire the scenery and to physically challenge themselves.

▲ Mount Everest lies in the Himalayas. Approximately five people die each year while trying to scale this mountain.

slopes, and have a small area at their summit. Mountains form over the course of millions of years. They are produced by movements in Earth's crust, which over time push an area of land higher.

Most mountains are part of ranges, with valleys separating the peaks. Lone mountains likely were once part of a range, but erosion slowly wore away the surrounding mountains. Major ranges include the Alps in Europe, the Andes in South America, and the Rocky Mountains in North America. The largest and highest mountains in the world are found in the Himalayas of Asia.

Mountains are barriers to wind. They force blowing air to rise up their slopes high into the atmosphere, where the air cools. At a mountain's summit, the temperature is cold and precipitation levels are high. Some very high mountains, including those in the Himalayas, are covered with ice and snow year-round.

MOUNTAIN WILDLIFE

Mountains are not hospitable to growing crops. They have low temperatures, and the soil on mountainsides is thin and stony. The soil is also too deficient in nitrogen to be productive in growing crops.

Mountains often have forests on the lower portions of their slopes. But trees cannot grow to their full size above the tree line. On upper slopes, vegetation is largely limited to grasses and shrubs. In tropical areas, plants can grow on mountains throughout the year, while in temperate areas, many

RAIN SHADOWS

In some regions, the two sides of a mountain might have very different climates. This is because of the rain shadow effect. On the windward side, which faces the wind, air travels up the slope, where it cools and produces rain and snow. After losing much of its moisture, the air warms as it passes over the mountain's leeward side, which is shielded from the wind. As a result, the wet windward side is thick with vegetation, while the arid leeward side can sustain only desert flora and fauna.

species can survive on mountains only in the summer. These plants often produce large flowers that coat the mountainside with brilliant colors.

Mountains are difficult environments for many animals, but some are able to make their homes there. Mountain meadows can be excellent pastures for sheep, cows, goats, and llamas. Large mammals such as deer, bears, and wolves are also acclimated to mountain habitats, although in cooler months they may migrate to lower altitudes. Some particularly hardy mammals, such as snow leopards and red pandas, are even able to thrive in the icy Himalayas.

CANYONS AND MESAS

The climate of other rocky terrains can be far different from that in cold mountainous regions. For instance, canyons are often found in arid or semiarid lands with hot and dry climates. Canyons are deep valleys with steep sides. They form when rivers cut through rock over time. Smaller canyons are often called gorges.

The most impressive canyons in the United States are found in the western portion of the country, the best-known being the Grand Canyon. The movement of Earth's crust lifted up the land that now forms the Colorado Plateau.

▲ Bighorn sheep can be found in canyons and on mountains alike.

Over the course of millions of years, the Colorado River flowed through this plateau and carved out the canyon. The Grand Canyon now teems with vegetation and wildlife. It is home to more than 1,700 species of plants and a variety of animals, including coyotes, squirrels, foxes, ravens, hawks, eagles, lizards, and toads.[1]

Other rocky terrains in the American West include mesas and buttes. Mesas are flat-topped hills with steep sides that rise high above the surrounding landscape. These rock formations were once part of a larger plateau that was worn away by erosion. Buttes are similar to mesas but smaller in size.

STORMY SKIES

While exploring dry canyons or snowy mountains, people may find themselves at the mercy of extreme weather. These weather conditions can lead to injury or even death. In the mountains, blizzards fill the air with snow, creating low visibility that can result in missteps and falls, possibly leading to fatal injuries. Lightning storms are also serious threats. Because lightning usually strikes the nearest high point in the landscape, people on mountain summits are at considerable risk of being killed during a lightning storm.

Unexpected heavy rainstorms spell danger in canyons. Rain flowing down into a canyon from elevated areas above can cause a flash flood. People exploring narrow-walled slot canyons are particularly vulnerable to being drowned by raging floodwaters.

EXTREME TEMPERATURES

In the mountains, storms that combine wind, snow, and very low temperatures place people at risk of hypothermia, a condition in which the body's internal temperature drops to dangerously low levels. Symptoms of hypothermia include shivering, drowsiness, stumbling, and slurred speech. The condition also affects the brain's ability to make rational decisions.

Extreme cold affects the tissue of the fingers, nose, toes, and ears. This can lead to the sensation of frostnip, which makes these extremities feel slightly numb. More prolonged exposure to low temperatures can lead to the more serious condition of frostbite. At its worst, frostbite results in the loss of all feeling, produces painful blisters, and turns the skin first gray and then black. Frostbite can damage tissue so severely that affected fingers and toes must be amputated.

Extreme heat can be just as stressful on the human body. With heat exhaustion, the body's temperature spikes, causing headaches, dizziness, and excessive sweating. If not relieved, it can escalate to heatstroke, which can lead to

> "Climb if you will, but remember that courage and strength are nought without prudence, and that a momentary negligence may destroy the happiness of a lifetime.[2]"
>
> —Edward Whymper, who became the first person to climb the Matterhorn, a famous mountain in the Alps, in 1865

▲ Climbers may need to carry supplemental oxygen if they are climbing at high elevations.

fevers as high as 104 degrees Fahrenheit (40ºC) and can cause a person to lose consciousness.³

Although the warmth of the sun can be welcome in the mountains, lengthy exposure to ultraviolet rays reflected off snow and ice can damage the eyes and result in snow blindness. Although snow blindness is usually temporary, the inability to see well can be catastrophic for a person trying to navigate mountainous terrain.

ALTITUDE SICKNESS AND DEHYDRATION

The atmosphere on and near mountain summits poses another serious health risk. Air at high altitudes is low in oxygen. Inadequate oxygen can lead to acute mountain sickness, characterized by headaches, exhaustion, nausea, and a lack of appetite. Another danger on mountaintops is high-altitude pulmonary edema, which is when fluid builds up in the lungs. This ailment leaves its victims with shortness of breath and a cough. High-altitude cerebral edema, in which a lack of oxygen causes the brain to swell, is a rare but very serious condition. This condition may result in fatigue, mental confusion, and sometimes even death.

People in hot and dry rocky terrains are especially susceptible to dehydration. This is a lack of water in the body that prevents it from functioning properly. But dehydration is also a risk for anyone venturing into mountainous regions.

Above 5,000 feet (1,520 m), the human respiratory system requires more frequent and deeper breaths.[4] Water from the lungs leaves the body with each breath exhaled, so heavy breathing contributes to dehydration. At high altitudes, people also urinate more often, removing even more fluid from the body. It is also easy for mountaineers to forget to drink enough water because high altitudes mask the usual signs of dehydration. Sweat evaporates quickly, and cold temperatures tend to suppress thirst.

FALLING DOWN

While navigating steep slopes, successful mountaineers are ever watchful for avalanches. An avalanche occurs when snow from a high area falls to a more level area. Avalanches can be triggered by the weather. A massive snowfall might leave so much snow that the top layers slide down. A rise in temperature can cause snow to melt, making it so heavy that it is pulled down by gravity. But the avalanches most likely to injure and kill are caused by the weight of humans traveling through mountainous terrain. More than 90 percent of avalanches that claim the lives of mountain climbers are triggered by the actions of their climbing party.[5]

In rocky environments, falling rock is an ever-present danger. Dramatic shifts in temperature, heavy rains, avalanches, and earthquakes can shake loose debris from rock faces and mountain slopes. Gravity then brings gravel and rocks crashing to

ROCKFALLS IN YOSEMITE

El Capitan is a rock formation in Yosemite National Park that stands 3,000 feet (910 m) tall. It might look rock solid, but on September 27, 2017, a huge slab fell off its eastern side near Waterfall Route, a popular area for rock climbers. Weighing 1,300 short tons (1,180 metric tons), the slab struck and killed a British tourist standing at El Capitan's base.[6] The following day, another rockfall injured a park visitor and created a cloud of dust so thick that it briefly blocked out sunlight in the area.

the ground. The size of a rockfall varies. It might rain pebbles or send giant boulders crashing down. Although rockfalls happen infrequently, they are hard to predict and are likely to cause injury or death to any person in their path.

Another risk is a person falling because of a misstep on a slick rocky surface, an icy patch, or a crumbling stone. Falls are responsible for most climbing accidents. While the majority leave climbers unharmed or with minor injuries, some lead to broken bones and other injuries requiring medical attention. As many as one in ten climbers injured in accidents are sent to the hospital.[7] But before they can be treated, many are faced with the daunting task of getting out of their threatening surroundings alive, either by a rescue effort or by finding a way to save themselves.

> **MOUNTAINS AND CLIMATE CHANGE**
>
> Because of climate change, mountainous regions are becoming more hazardous places. Extreme fluctuations in temperatures are causing more avalanches. As the planet warms, mountain glaciers are melting at a faster rate, which results in frequent flooding. The retreating glaciers also expose the land underneath to erosion, increasing the risk of landslides. Because the exposed land is darker than ice, it absorbs more heat from the sun, which only speeds up the warming of the landscape.

CHAPTER 3

OVER THE MOUNTAIN

After learning Chile had suspended its rescue mission, the survivors of the Uruguayan plane crash realized they had to save themselves. Their first plan was to send an expedition of their strongest, healthiest men to find the tail that had broken off the plane. In the tail, there were batteries that might be able to power the plane's radio system, allowing them to call for help.

UP THE MOUNTAIN

Gustavo Zerbino, Numa Turcatti, and Daniel Maspons were chosen for the task. They immediately headed out and began to scale the mountain that lay to the

◀ Survivors from the Uruguayan plane crash huddled in the body of the plane for warmth.

west of the fuselage. Those below watched as they struggled to climb its face, which at some spots was almost vertical. One saving grace was the afternoon sun. Even though they had only light jackets, the sunshine kept them warm.

But as the sun was going down, Zerbino, Turcatti, and Maspons had made it only halfway up the mountain. They could either abandon the mission or settle in for the night and keep going the next day. They decided to sleep on the mountain but were unprepared for the severe cold. Fearing they would not survive the night, the men took turns hitting one another to keep their blood circulating.

After sunrise, the young men continued their climb. They did not find the tail, though they did make a grim discovery. Their path was strewn with the bodies of the passengers who had been sucked out of the plane when the tail was ripped off. When the men returned empty-handed to the fuselage, the other

BLIND IN THE SNOW

When descending the mountain after the futile search for the plane's tail, Gustavo Zerbino's broken sunglasses slipped down his nose, leaving his eyes vulnerable to bright light reflected off the snow. He then fell victim to snow blindness. By the time Zerbino reached the fuselage, he was nearly blind. He spent the next two days with a rugby shirt over his eyes to give them time to heal.

survivors were shocked at their physical condition after their grueling ordeal.

THE EXPEDITIONERS

The survivors were all demoralized by the failed expedition. But on October 29, their seventeenth day on the mountain, they experienced an even greater disaster. That night, as they were trying to sleep in the fuselage, they heard a loud rumbling that sounded like a horse stampede. Suddenly, an avalanche of snow filled the plane. Everyone began digging to free themselves and others before being smothered. Despite their frantic efforts, eight people died in the avalanche, including Pérez and Liliana Methol, the only

▼ Avalanche snow can travel faster than the speed of cars on a freeway. Large chunks of ice can hit and kill people, or people can become buried.

woman who had survived to that point. It took the nineteen survivors eight days to dig the hard snow and corpses out of the plane.

After the avalanche, the survivors were more determined than ever to save themselves. They planned an expedition, during which four men would climb the mountain to the west and head into Chile to find help. The weather was still too harsh to send out the group. But by late November, the summer weather in the Southern Hemisphere would melt some snow, making the trek easier.

In the meantime, the four chosen expeditioners—Parrado, Turcatti, Canessa, and Antonio Vizintín—received special privileges so they build up their strength. They were excused from chores, such as making water from snow and cleaning up the fuselage. They were also allowed to sleep wherever and whenever they wanted and received extra rations of meat.

FINDING THE TAIL

On November 17, Parrado, Canessa, and Vizintín set out, leaving Turcatti behind because a wound on his leg had developed a severe infection. Early on their journey, they came upon the plane's tail. Inside, they found the batteries in working order. Near the tail, they also found other supplies, including clothing, from passengers' suitcases.

After a warm night in the tail, the expeditioners continued their trek. But Canessa started having doubts. He argued that they should turn around, return to the fuselage, and try to fix the plane's radio with the batteries they found. Vizintín agreed, and Parrado reluctantly went along.

The group tinkered with the plane's radio, but even with the batteries, they could not get it to work. The survivors, however, had a new reason for hope. On their transistor radio, they heard a report that a new rescue mission had been launched.

Canessa said they should wait for the rescue plane, but the others wanted the expeditioners to make the planned trek to Chile. Parrado was particularly insistent. He knew that if they did not get off the mountain soon, they would be forced to eat the bodies of his

TREASURES ON THE MOUNTAIN

When the expeditioners located the airplane's tail, they found something else almost as exciting—suitcases that had been strewn in the snow when the plane crashed. The men scoured through the suitcases like they were on a treasure hunt. They found plenty of clothes, sweets, sodas, and even a camera loaded with film. But they were particularly excited about a photograph of a little girl at a birthday party. They loved looking at the picture and imagining what her birthday cake tasted like.

sister and mother. Then Turcatti, formerly one of the fittest of the group, died, finally convincing Canessa that the expeditioners needed to go on their self-rescue mission.

HEADING OUT

In the early morning of December 12, everyone emerged from the plane to wish Parrado, Canessa, and Vizintín good luck on their journey. The three men were dressed in multiple layers of clothing salvaged from the dead and from suitcases found lying near the tail. They also carried a warm sleeping bag crafted from insulation torn from the tail's heating system. Before leaving, Parrado gave those staying behind permission to consume his family members' bodies if they had to.

The first day, the climb was difficult. Vizintín's toes were rubbed raw as the men scaled the mountain. While climbing, Parrado loosened some rocks, which almost hit Canessa below him. Canessa cried out, "Are you trying to kill me?"[1] When the sun set, they spent an uncomfortable night on a snowy ledge after struggling to find a place to sleep.

The next morning Canessa wanted to turn around, but Parrado and Vizintín insisted on pressing on to the summit. Canessa soon joined them. They had expected to see a

▲ Parrado, *left*, and Canessa, *center*, continued on the journey, committed to finding help for themselves and the remaining survivors.

grassy valley below. But instead there was only more ice. Canessa said, "There isn't a chance . . . of getting through that."[2] The only reason for hope was two small summits without snow that pointed to a way out of the Andes. They realized they did not have the food supplies to sustain three men during the long hike ahead, so Vizintín returned to the plane.

During their descent, Parrado decided to try sledding down on a seat cushion. His sled flew down the slope and threw him into a snowbank. After all they had been through, Canessa could not believe his friend had just been so reckless. But to his relief, Parrado emerged from the snow uninjured.

SIGNS OF LIFE

After reaching the valley, Parrado and Canessa continued their seemingly endless trek. Day after day, they walked for miles, not even sure where they were headed. Occasionally, there were encouraging signs—a patch of grass, a lizard skittering along the ground, or a tin can. Even so, by the ninth day, Canessa said he did not have the strength to go on. Parrado encouraged Canessa onward.

Near sunset on December 20, Canessa spied three herdsmen on the other side of a river. Parrado and Canessa began yelling and wildly waving their arms, but the herdsmen could not hear them over the water's roar. One of the herdsmen shouted he would come back tomorrow and rode away.

Early the next morning, a herdsman returned and threw across the river a pen and paper attached to a rock. Parrado wrote a note explaining they were survivors of the plane crash and begged for help.

> "I come from a plane that fell in the mountains. I am Uruguayan. . . . In the plane there are still 14 injured people. . . . We don't have any food. We are weak. When are you going to come and fetch us?[3]"
>
> —from Parrado's note to the herdsman he and Canessa encountered after their ten-day journey

With barely any strength left, he managed to throw it to the opposite bank. The herdsman read the note and headed off to the nearest town to alert the authorities. While he was away, other herdsmen arrived and took Parrado and Canessa to a hunting camp, where they were fed a meal of beans, macaroni, and meat. The police arrived that night accompanied by reporters. When the reporters asked the men what they had eaten at the crash site, Parrado and Canessa dodged the question.

▼ Sergio Catalán, *center*, was the herdsman who rode to alert authorities of the survivors. He remained in touch with some of the survivors for the rest of his life.

THE MIRACLE OF THE ANDES

On December 22 and 23, helicopters arrived to rescue the rest of the survivors from their 71-day ordeal. The survival story, called the Miracle of the Andes, became international news. The media hailed the survivors as heroes. But after learning they had survived by eating human flesh, there was an immediate backlash in the press. Sensationalist stories recast them as immoral villains for their actions.

The survivors challenged this public condemnation. On December 28, they held a news conference in Montevideo, Uruguay. Survivor Alfredo Delgado explained how the story of Jesus at the Last Supper had informed their actions. "It was this that helped us to survive," he said, "and now we do not want this—which for us was something intimate, intimate—to be hackneyed or touched or anything like that."[4] His words put an end to the harshest news stories about their experiences in the Andes.

PLAYING THE GAME

It took 40 years, but the rugby team finally got to play a match in Chile in 2012. Now in their late fifties and early sixties, survivors from the Old Christians team traveled to Santiago to compete against former players of the Old Grangonian, the Chilean team they were supposed to play when their plane went down. During the game, the players and the crowd paid tribute to the Old Christians who had died in the crash and on the mountain as their relatives wept in the stands.

The book *Alive: The Story of the Andes Survivors*, a 1974 account of their struggles written by Piers Paul Read, also helped restore the survivors' reputations. The best-selling book was made into a movie in 1993 starring Ethan Hawke as Parrado and Josh Hamilton as Canessa. Some survivors wrote memoirs. Parrado's *Miracle in the Andes* was published in 2006, and Canessa's *I Had to Survive* was released in 2016.

In 2006, the two men joined other survivors in returning to the mountain to film *Stranded,* a documentary in which they were interviewed about their memories of being stranded in the Andes. The 2007 film was directed by Gonzalo Arijón, who had been a childhood friend of many of the rugby players. In the film's closing moments, Canessa says, sitting at the crash site decades later, that he can still feel the presence of the dead: "I think they're in the air. They float. They're floating around us. . . . They still whisper in our ears."[5]

CHAPTER 4

DESCENDING THE OGRE

On July 13, 1977, Doug Scott marveled at the landscape of mountains and glaciers around him, knowing he was the first person to view them from his vantage point. He had just ascended Baintha Brakk, a mountain in the Pakistani part of the Karakoram Range. The mountain stands 23,000 feet (7,000 m) tall, and no one had ever before reached the summit of this tower of stone and ice, known to climbers by the nickname the Ogre.[1]

Soon Scott's climbing partner Chris Bonington joined him. They were part of a six-member British climbing expedition Scott had organized. Bonington and Scott were the most experienced of the

◀ The Ogre is a difficult mountain to climb. After the first successful summit in 1977, it was 24 years until another team successfully reached the top.

six mountaineers. Both were already well known for having climbed Mount Everest, the world's highest mountain.

Two less experienced climbers on the expedition—Julian "Mo" Anthoine and Clive Rowland—had climbed most of the way up, but they were unsure if they had the skills to reach the summit. They waited at a snow cave below for Scott and Bonington's return. The two other climbers—Paul "Tut" Braithwaite and Nick Estcourt—were at base camp at the bottom of the Ogre. Braithwaite's leg had been injured by a falling rock, and he was unable to climb. Estcourt had almost made it to the top with Bonington days before, but he was too exhausted to risk making another attempt.

BROKEN LEGS

Almost as soon as Bonington joined Scott on the summit, Scott insisted they had to start their descent. It was seven o'clock in the evening, and they had to get to the snow cave before sunset. Scott prepared to rappel down the steep rock wall below them.

With his feet on the rock, Scott drew himself downward using a rope. A cold wind was blowing, and a thin layer of ice had formed over the snow. Hurrying down, Scott did not notice an ice patch. When his feet hit it, they slid into the air. His body twisted around as he frantically tried to regain control. Before he could, his body slammed against the rock face. "I came to a stop," he later recalled, "bouncing on the end of the rope, every bone shaken."[2] Bonington was still enjoying the view atop the Ogre when he heard what he later called "a Tarzan-like yell." It was followed by a chilling shout: "I've broken my legs."[3]

Bonington rappelled down and found Scott sitting on a small ledge. After Scott told him what happened, Bonington urged him not to panic. "We'll get you down somehow," he said.[4] Despite his calming words, Bonington was upset. He had no idea how they were going get Scott down the Ogre.

> My feet slid across the ice, off into the air and away I went. . . . I twisted and turned in an effort to face squarely, great cracked walls of rock streaked with snow looming up fast—on and on, zooming in, with my boots in front of me like a pair of buffers—no stopping it now.[5]
>
> —Doug Scott, describing the accident that broke his legs

CAUGHT IN A STORM

It was now too dark to get to the snow cave, so their immediate problem was finding a place to spend the night.

Bonington saw a patch of snow below that he could dig out to create a sleeping platform. Scott followed him down, touching the mountain with his back instead of his feet. The maneuver worked well until he reached the platform, where, without thinking about it, he put his whole weight on his feet, causing him immense pain.

At first light, they rappelled down frozen ropes to the snow cave. Anthoine and Rowland, who had seen Scott's accident, had dug out steps in the snow on the path to the cave. Scott managed to crawl down the steps on his knees. Wrapped in their sleeping bags, Scott and Bonington rested all day. The four men ate the last food they had with them—a soup thickened with mashed potato powder.

The next morning, they woke to find the entrance of their cave filled with snow. Afraid of suffocating, they quickly

ONE STEP AT A TIME

Throughout his harrowing descent down the Ogre, Doug Scott worried that if he survived, the injuries to his legs would put an end to his favorite pastimes of mountain climbing and playing rugby. But he knew dwelling on such negative thoughts would keep him from focusing on what he had to do to get off the mountain. Instead, he tried to think only of each small step he had to make toward that goal, such as crossing the next snow basin, to keep up his spirits.

dug it out only to find a snowstorm was raging outside. They had no food, and they were worried about how the high altitude would affect their bodies. But as the snow fell and the wind blew, they had no choice but to stay in the snow cave another day and night.

ANOTHER ACCIDENT

Even though snow was still falling, the men set out again. The best route required them to climb up and over the Ogre's west summit. Scott had figured out how to rappel

▼ Climbing and descending a mountain is challenging even without an injury. Crampons on shoes help keep climbers from slipping.

▲ Estcourt, *left*, and Bonington, *right*, had climbed the Himalayan mountain Brammah together in 1973.

downward in his injured state, but ascending was another matter. He had to rely on just his hands and arms to pull himself up the rope. Rowland and Anthoine went first, followed by Scott, with Bonington bringing up the rear. Scott grew weak during the six-hour climb. Rowland and Anthoine had to pull him up the last 70 feet (21 m).[6]

After spending the night in another snow cave, the four men set out to rappel down the rock face known as the Red Pillar. It was now Bonington's turn to run out of luck. Because of a problem with the ropes, he suddenly dropped 20 feet (6 m) before he was able to steady himself. As he fell, he hit a rock with what he later called "a terrifying crunch."[7]

His ribcage felt bruised, but otherwise Bonington thought he had emerged from the accident unscathed.

FROM CAMP TO CAMP

That night they reached Camp III, where, after removing three feet (0.9 m) of snow, they could at last shelter in tents.[8] The mood was light as the men played cards and listened to music on a tape recording. Bonington, however, was struggling. He was coughing and could barely speak. Even worse, he felt sharp pain with every cough, which made him realize that his collision with the rock had broken several ribs.

The following morning, Bonington was in a panic. He was sure he had pulmonary edema and needed immediate medical attention. Anthoine was less convinced. He reminded Bonington that he had been at high altitudes plenty of times before without getting altitude sickness.

"Don't worry, Chris," Anthoine joked. "It's probably only pneumonia"—a diagnosis that was later proved correct.[9] After Bonington calmed down, they decided to spend the day in the tents and ride out the last of the storm. After not eating for four days, they were cheered by the discovery of a box of sugar cubes and a few used teabags scattered at the camp site.

When the snowstorm cleared, the men rappelled to Camp II, where they hoped at last to find food. But there was nothing but a little milk powder, fruit candy, cough lozenges, and frozen cooked rice. As they shared their meager meal, they comforted themselves with the fact that they were only a day away from base camp, where they would meet up with Braithwaite and Estcourt and finally get a real meal.

CRAWLING TO BASE CAMP

By the next afternoon, the men reached a glacier. They were only a three-mile (5 km) walk from base camp.[10] Anthoine and Bonington went ahead, while Rowland stayed behind with Scott, who had to crawl on his hands and knees the entire way. He wore several pairs of pants to protect his knees from rocks and gravel, but still the trek was grueling. As the sun fell, Rowland insisted on going to base camp on his own, promising to come back with food and a headlight. Even with base camp ever closer, Scott despaired as he continued his slow crawl alone under a starry sky.

When Rowland returned, he brought muesli bars and sugar cubes, along with some disheartening news. Braithwaite and Estcourt had left base camp for Askole, a small village 30 miles (48 km) away.[11] Braithwaite had abandoned the camp earlier, while Estcourt had stayed until that morning. Estcourt left behind a note but had no real hope that the four climbers would ever see it. Braithwaite and Estcourt were sure the others had all died, defeated by the Ogre. The note said Braithwaite and Estcourt planned to return soon with help, expecting they would have to search for bodies. Just in case, though, they had left behind a modest store of food under a boulder, where it was safe from hungry bears.

His knees swollen and bloody, Scott, along with Rowland, finally reached base camp at about three o'clock in the morning. They found Bonington there alone. Antholne had gone off in search of Estcourt, who was likely still en route to Askole. After a meal of cake and tea, Scott fell into a deep sleep. Forty years later, he wrote about how he felt as he woke up the next day, at last off

CLEAN WATER FOR ASKOLE

During his last mountaineering trip to Pakistan in 1990, Doug Scott found out that the drinking water in the village of Askole was highly polluted. As a result, more than half of the village's children died before reaching adulthood. Grateful for all the aid the people of Askole had given him while climbing the Ogre and other nearby mountains, Scott became determined to help them. He used his notoriety in the British mountaineering community to raise funds for a pipeline that brought fresh spring water to the village.

the mountain and safe: "Poking my head out to see the grass, flowers, and the stream, brewing a mug of tea, and feeling the sun burning my skin are beautiful memories I will never lose."[12]

Anthoine meanwhile continued his search for Estcourt. He walked for a day and a half, stopping only for catnaps. Twice, he fell asleep while walking. Finally, he got to Askole. Trudging up a hill, he spied Estcourt, who was delighted to see his friend was still alive.

A HELICOPTER RESCUE

Four days passed as Scott, Bonington, and Rowland waited impatiently at base camp, wondering if anyone was coming to help them. Finally, on the fifth morning, Estcourt marched into the campsite with a team of hired porters from Askole. They built a stretcher for Scott out of wooden poles. The porters and climbers then set out on the long hike to the village.

Just outside Askole, the porters left the climbers in a flat pasture. Half an hour later, a helicopter arrived. All three men wanted to get aboard. Scott and Bonington had been in desperate need of medical attention for days, while Rowland was suffering from a severe case of frostbite. But the helicopter pilot said he could take only one at a time. He got Scott into the vehicle and told the others he would be back in a few hours.

Days passed as Bonington and Rowland waited in the village. After all the pain and stress on the Ogre, Bonington later said that this wait was the worst part of the entire ordeal as he was overcome by

OLD MAN OF HOY

Perhaps the most famous mountaineer in the United Kingdom, Chris Bonington celebrated his eightieth birthday in 2014 by climbing the Old Man of Hoy—a 449-foot (137 m) sea stack off the northern coast of Scotland.[14] Bonington had first ascended the Old Man in 1966. In 1967, he again climbed the famous landmark with six other mountaineers as an audience of 15 million watched them on live television.[15] Known as the Great Climb, the event helped popularize mountaineering in the United Kingdom.

a desperate boredom. He later found out why the helicopter had not returned. As it was landing near a medical facility, its engine cut out 20 feet (6 m) off the ground.[13] The helicopter crashed, but neither Scott nor the pilot was injured. After surviving his trek down the Ogre with two broken legs, Scott could have been killed in a helicopter crash if the engine had failed just a few minutes earlier.

After six days, another helicopter finally came for Bonington. It flew him to Islamabad, the capital of Pakistan, where Bonington had friends at the British Embassy. The best place to land near the embassy was a golf course.

As Bonington later remembered, he emerged from the helicopter looking like "a bearded filthy skeleton, clad in . . . a dirty blue sweater, clutching an ice axe." Bonington noted that the "golfers kept their distance whilst I waited for someone from the Embassy to pick me up."[16]

With all its twists and turns, the survival story of Scott and Bonington became one of the greatest and most-told tales in British mountaineering history. Scott later regretted that Rowland and Anthoine's roles were often ignored in favor of the more famous stories of Scott and Bonington. Bonington particularly became associated with the Ogre survival story because he frequently appeared on British television. In interviews, however, he always balked when people claimed he had conquered the Ogre. As he explained, "I felt that the Ogre had allowed us to climb it and then, like a great cat, had played with us all the way down, finally allowing us to escape, mauled but in one piece to play more games with other mountains in the future."[17]

▲ Scott continued climbing after facing the Ogre. He forged a new, challenging path on the third-highest mountain, Kangchenjunga in the Himalayas, in 1979.

CHAPTER 5

THE END OF
THE ROPE

Joe Simpson and Simon Yates were up for a challenge. Both in their early twenties, the young English mountaineers had climbed numerous peaks in the Alps. But they were now hungry to ascend higher mountains, especially ones whose summits no one had ever reached.

A friend who had climbed extensively in South America told them about Siula Grande in the Andes Mountains of Peru. Nobody had ever ascended the west face of this peak that stands 21,000 feet (6,400 m) high, though several had tried.[1] Taking on Siula Grande excited Simpson. Yates was also convinced they could succeed where other climbers had failed.

◀ The west face of Siula Grande, *pictured*, is steeper than the north ridge, which was first summited in 1936.

TO THE SUMMIT

In early June 1985, after a two-day trek from the nearest road, Simpson and Yates reached the base of Siula Grande. With them was Richard Hawking, a young man they met in the Peruvian capital of Lima. Eager for adventure, Hawking took them up on their invitation to come along. Hawking was not a mountaineer, but he agreed to take care of base camp while his two new friends were on the mountain.

The first day of the climb, Simpson and Yates were full of confidence. The second day, they were less sure about their success. It started to snow, and the flakes were so powdery they stuck on the mountaineers' clothing and froze. Both felt as though they were wearing a suit of armor. The powdery snow was also unstable, making it difficult to keep their footing. After an exhausting day, they dug out a snow cave to spend the night.

The two men continued, even as they struggled to stay

> "We were fairly anarchic and fairly irresponsible, and we didn't give a d— about anyone else or anything else, and we just wanted to climb the world. And it was fun. It was just brilliant fun. And every now and then it went wildly wrong. And then it wasn't.[2]"
>
> —Simpson on his and Yates's youthful enthusiasm for mountain climbing

hydrated in the high altitude. They had not melted enough snow to make an adequate supply of drinking water. After three days of difficult and dangerous climbing, they finally reached the summit.

Even with clouds heading toward them from the west, they thought their route might help them reach base camp before sunset. But soon after descending the summit, they found themselves lost in the clouds. As dark set in, they decided to spend another night on Siula Grande. That night, they exhausted their supply of gas, which they used to melt snow.

> ## CLIMBING ALPINE STYLE
>
> When scaling Siula Grande, Simpson and Yates used a climbing method known as Alpine style. Traditional mountaineering makes use of numerous campsites stocked with food, supplies, and supplemental oxygen along the climbing route. Pioneered in the 1970s, Alpine style does away with fixed camps. Climbers instead carry packs with all their own clothing, food, and equipment and try to make the climb in one big push. Yates explains, "There's no helicopter rescue and there's no other people.... If you get badly hurt, you'll probably die."[3]

DISASTER ON SIULA GRANDE

At first light, they resumed their descent, sure they would soon reach base camp. Yates later said, "I thought at that stage, it was pretty much in the bag I suppose, the

▲ In cold climates, outdoor adventurers need to bring a small camping stove, fuel, and a fuel canister to melt snow for drinking water. They should also bring a filter to purify the water.

whole climb." Simpson was ahead, out of Yates's view, when he took a misstep. He suddenly felt terrible pain in his knee and thigh. "I can't have broken my leg," Simpson thought. "If I have broken my leg, I'm dead."[4] He frantically felt his leg, but finding no blood, he thought maybe he had just torn a ligament. He tried putting weight on his ailing leg. A burst of terrible pain told him his leg was definitely broken.

As Yates approached his friend, he saw on Simpson's face a "look of shock and desperation and a sort of terror." Simpson was sure Yates was going to continue without him and that he would die alone on the mountain. For a moment, Yates thought of how much simpler the situation would be if Simpson simply slipped off the mountainside so he would not "have all the hassle of trying to deal with him and the situation we're in."[5] Then, to Simpson's relief, Yates started strategizing with him about what to do next.

Following the plan they developed, Yates dug out a seat in the snow in which he could sit securely. They tied the two ends of a 330-foot (100 m) rope around their bodies.[6] Yates then used the rope to lower Simpson down the slope.

When the rope was fully released, Yates shook it a little as a signal to Simpson. Simpson was supposed to then secure himself so he would not fall, making the rope less taut. Yates then knew to climb down to meet up with Simpson. Repeating the process over and over in a raging storm, they managed to descend another 3,000 feet (910 m) before Simpson slipped off a cliff.[7] He suddenly found himself dangling in the air over a crevasse in the glacier below.

A DIFFICULT DECISION

Unable to see or hear Simpson, Yates was puzzled when he shook the rope to signal Simpson and it remained taut. He waited for more than an hour, having no idea what was going on. Yates then felt the powdery snow underneath him begin to give way. If he did nothing, his snow seat would collapse, and he would be sent flying off the mountain to a certain death. Yates thought about his options and realized there was only one. He pulled a Swiss army knife out of his pack and cut the rope.

The next morning, Yates continued down Siula Grande alone. He found the cliff and realized what had happened. Yates shouted down toward the crevasse, but he knew it was hopeless. Simpson was surely dead. On the way to base

▼ Mountaineers usually travel with a rope tied to at least one partner to prevent one of them from falling into a crevasse.

camp, he thought about what he would tell their friends and Simpson's parents. He considered lying about what happened so no one would think badly of him. But when he reached the camp and Hawking asked where Simpson was, Yates blurted out the truth. Hawking seemed to understand that he had had no choice, but the death of Simpson and his part in it continued to haunt Yates.

IN THE CREVASSE

Yates did not know that after he had cut the rope, Simpson did indeed plunge into the deep crevasse below. But he had landed on a ledge rather than falling all the way down. Simpson later explained, "If I had landed five feet [1.5 m] to the left and gone down that big hole, I'd just have disappeared."[8] After Simpson realized where he was and what had happened, he gingerly tugged on the rope, expecting to pull down Yates' dead body. Instead he reeled in a rope with an obviously cut end. Simpson then knew Yates

> **It was dark, and it began to get to me. There is something about crevasses, they have a dread feel, not the place for the living. I could hear the ice cracking, and wind noises in the ice.... I felt very, very alone. And I was very scared.[9]**
>
> —*Simpson on his night trapped in a crevasse*

was still alive. He called out frantically to him but received no response.

When the sun rose, Simpson tried climbing out of the crevasse, but with his broken leg it was impossible. However, he could rappel down, deeper into the crevasse. The thought terrified him. But he could either stay where he was and die or climb down and search for an escape route. As he used his ropes to lower himself, he saw what he thought was the crevasse's floor covered in snow. To one side, a slope led to a hole through which the sun was streaming. As Simpson crawled toward the hole, the snow underneath him began to crack. Escaping the collapsing snow floor, he managed to get through the hole and onto the glacier outside. Relieved to still be alive, Simpson laid on the glacier as the sun warmed his face. Simpson laughed. He then remembered he was many miles from base camp.

THE TREK TO BASE CAMP

Simpson started down the glacier, using his hands and good leg to slide his body down the ice. To distract himself from the long distance he had to go, he set small goals, challenging himself to reach a spot ahead within 20 minutes. The route down became more challenging when he reached an area filled with rocks and boulders. Simpson then had to move by hopping on his good leg. With almost every hop, he fell on his broken leg, collapsing in agony.

After two days and nights, Simpson woke up with the sun on his face. He had the comforting idea that he would just stay there and die. There was no point in continuing because by then Yates and Hawking had undoubtedly packed up base camp and left. But Simpson decided to try to reach the camp on the off chance he could see his friends again because he realized he did not want to die by himself.

Yates and Hawking were in fact still at base camp. Worried about Yates's mental state, Hawking urged him to leave. Finally, they decided to abandon the camp the next morning. To lighten their load, they burned Simpson's clothing—an act that felt like a funeral for their dead friend.

SNOW AND HYDRATION

During Simpson's struggle to return to base camp, he suffered from extreme dehydration, even though he was surrounded by snow. Experienced outdoor athletes know that eating snow is not an effective way of hydrating the human body. The body uses a great deal of energy to turn snow into water, and it draws on its own water stores to create that energy. Eating too much snow in an emergency situation, therefore, can lead to fatigue and even dehydrate the body further.

⚠ More mountain injuries happen descending mountains than ascending them, in part because of fatigue and because climbers focus more on reaching the top than going down.

REUNION

By nightfall, Simpson began hallucinating. He later remembered little of the night, except for a ridiculous pop song that played over and over in his head, making him feel like he was losing his mind. At about one o'clock in the morning, he smelled a stench that he struggled to identify. Suddenly, he realized he had crawled through the area near base camp that they had used as a latrine.

Yates and Hawking woke to an anguished cry: "Simon!" They rushed from their tent to find what seemed like a ghost in the dark night. Yates ran to Simpson and hugged him. Simpson thanked Yates for trying to get him off the mountain. He assured Yates he was right to cut the rope, saying, "I'd have done the same."[10] After traveling two days by donkey and one day in the back of a pickup, the three men made it to Lima. There, Simpson received medical care before heading back to England.

AFTERMATH

Simpson's doctors told him he would never walk again. But after multiple surgeries, he was able to not only walk but also to return to climbing, though he became more careful. Only a few weeks after returning home, Yates was again climbing mountains. But he was dogged by disapproval within the British climbing community for cutting his rope on Siula Grande.

In part to restore Yates's reputation, Simpson wrote *Touching the Void,* an account of their expedition. The book's dedication reads, "To Simon Yates, for a debt I can never repay."[11] *Touching the Void* went on to sell more than one million copies.[12] It also inspired a 2003 documentary film and a play that began running on London's West End in 2019. Since the publication of *Touching the Void,* Simpson has become a successful writer of both fiction and nonfiction.

In a 2019 interview, Simpson mused that if he had not "had that experience in Peru, I would never have become a writer, which I love." At the same time, he regretted that his injuries had limited his mountaineering career, leading him to ponder "what if?" But Simpson in the end concluded, "Actually, the most likely 'what if' is that I'd be dead."[13]

ENDING ON A HIGH NOTE

In 2009, Simpson sat atop a mountain in Nepal. He had a spectacular view of Everest, Lhotse, and many other great peaks. "It doesn't get much better than this," he thought.[14] The moment was spoiled, though, when he remembered he would spend the next three days in terrible pain as he made his descent. His years of climbing had severely injured his back, his ankles, and most of all, his right knee. Simpson then told himself this would be his last climb. When he got off the mountain, he sold his gear and retired from climbing.

▲ Simpson climbed cliffs in Derbyshire, United Kingdom, four years after surviving Siula Grande.

CHAPTER 6

TRAPPED BY A BOULDER

On the morning of Saturday, April 26, 2003, Aron Ralston woke up in the back of his truck, ready for the day's adventure. The night before, he had camped out at the trailhead of Horseshoe Canyon in Utah so he could get an early start. Ralston was supposed to be on a five-day mountain-climbing vacation with some friends, but the trip was canceled at the last minute.

Ralston then decided to spend his planned time off alone exploring the desert lands of Utah. When he went into the wilderness, he usually left a detailed itinerary with his roommates. But this time, he decided to figure out his trip a day at a time, without a set agenda in mind.

◀ Canyonlands National Park contains many canyons and other rock formations, such as the Needles.

Ralston had taken up mountain climbing after graduating from college. Working as a mechanical engineer, he spent his free time indulging his passion for adventure sports. Soon Ralston became so committed to a life of outdoor adventure that he quit his engineering job and moved to Aspen, Colorado, in 2002. While working in a mountaineering equipment store to make ends meet, he devoted most of his time to hiking, biking, and climbing.

GOING SOLO

Ralston's adventures often put him in danger. For instance, he was hit by an avalanche while skiing down Resolution Mountain in Colorado after being warned of hazardous weather conditions. For him, the outing he planned for his Saturday in Utah was relatively tame. He decided to mountain bike 15 miles (24 km) to the

A DANGEROUS THRILL

Ralston was enthralled by the IMAX movie *Everest* (1998), which told the story of a group of mountaineers struggling to scale the world's highest peak. Then living in Arizona, Ralston was inspired to set out the next day to climb Humphreys Peak, the highest point in the state. As he climbed, he found himself in the middle of a lightning storm. He later remembered that he could see "blue zaps going back and forth" between the tips of the hiking poles he was using to steady himself as he climbed."[1] What might have terrified another novice climber thrilled Ralston. All he wanted was to experience that feeling again.

entrance of Bluejohn Canyon. Ralston would then descend into the canyon, exploring it along a 13-mile (21 km) route before biking back to his truck.[2] He estimated that the expedition would take about eight hours.

Before leaving, Ralston loaded his backpack with everything he would need. It held his canyoneering gear, including a rope and harness he would use to rappel down a 65-foot (20 m) rock wall nicknamed the Big Drop.[3] He brought two burritos and four candy bars to eat.[4] And he packed one gallon (3.8 L) of water to stay hydrated.[5] Along with his headphones and CD player, he packed a video camera to record what he saw. He did not bring a mobile phone because there was no phone reception in the deep canyon.

> ### BLUE JOHN
> Utah's Bluejohn Canyon got its name through its association with Blue John Griffith, who had one blue eye and one brown eye. During the late 1800s, Griffith was a cook and horse thief who hid out in the remote area. He often worked with the Wild Bunch, the notorious criminal gang led by Butch Cassidy. After barely surviving a shootout with lawmen, Griffith gave up his life of crime. In late 1899 he left his hideout and traveled down the Colorado River. What happened to him after that is now lost to history.

STUCK AND DESPERATE

Seven miles (11 km) into the canyon, Ralston came upon a chockstone—a boulder stuck between two canyon walls.

▲ As a teenager, Aron Ralston enjoyed hiking and backpacking and eventually added more ambitious activities.

He had to get around the chockstone and down to the canyon floor about 12 feet (3.7 m) below.[6] After kicking the stone a few times to make sure it was firmly in place, he dangled off it with his hands before preparing to fall to the floor. After Ralston felt the chockstone move slightly, he immediately let go. But his body weight had already loosened the 800-pound (360 kg) boulder.[7] It came crashing down, pinning his right hand and forearm to the canyon wall.

The pain was excruciating. Ralston later likened it to the feeling of slamming a finger in a car door, only 100 times worse. But pain was far from his biggest problem. Unable to pull out his hand, he was now trapped in a tight space between two canyon walls. In a panic, he threw his body against the stone, but it did not budge.

Ralston told himself to calm down and reason through the situation. He thought about waiting to be rescued but then remembered that no one knew where he was. He became furious with himself for not leaving behind an itinerary as any serious climber or hiker knew to do. Ralston also realized that the area was so remote that no other hiker was likely to spot him by chance. He was so deep in the canyon that even if a rescue helicopter were overhead, he could not be seen.

WEIGHING THE OPTIONS

That night, unable to sleep, Ralston stayed up scraping at the rock with a three-inch (8 cm) blade on the small multi-tool he had packed.[8] As Sunday dawned, he gave up on that. He tried using his climbing equipment to construct a pulley system to lift the boulder, but that proved just as futile. Convinced he was doomed, Ralston pulled out his video camera to tape his last will and testament, in which he gave away his belongings to his friends and family.

On Monday, Ralston decided to consider an option he had avoided thinking about—amputation. He fashioned a tourniquet from the tubing of an empty water bottle. If he cut off his hand, the tight tourniquet around his arm could keep him from quickly bleeding to death. With the tourniquet in place, he tried sawing his arm using his tool's three-inch (8 cm) blade, but it was too dull.[9]

With no food or water left, he tried again on Tuesday. This time, he stabbed his arm with the tool's smaller and sharper 1.5-inch (4 cm) blade.[10] After penetrating the flesh, he moved the blade around until it hit the bone. Ralston felt a wave of despair. He might be able to slice his skin and muscle. But there was no way the little blade could cut through bone.

> "That boulder had probably seen hundreds of people climb over it since it had been wedged there however many eons ago. For whatever reason, when I tried to climb off it, it moved. I think the boulder was put there to teach me something."[11]
>
> —Ralston, on how his experiences in Bluejohn Canyon changed him, 2003

TAKING ACTION

On Wednesday, he gave up and prepared to die. He was comforted by hallucinations he had of his friends. He even thought he heard the voice of his mother calling out to him. As the temperature dropped sharply, he became convinced he would not survive the night. Ralston then fell into a dream. He saw a little blond boy whom he recognized as his future son. He also saw himself, with a stump where his right hand had

▼ People can still see the rock, *second from top*, that trapped Ralston in Bluejohn Canyon.

been, happily playing with the boy. When Ralston woke, he suddenly realized that somehow, he was going to live. "That belief, that boy, change[d] everything for me," he later said.[12]

On Thursday morning, Ralston looked at his pinned hand and felt disgusted. Its blood circulation cut off, it was now gray, rotting flesh. "It's not part of me," he thought. "It's garbage."[13] He began to flail his body until he felt his pinned arm bending unnaturally. The bones had grown brittle due to lack of blood flow. He pushed hard on it with his left hand. Two bones snapped just above the wrist. Ralston pulled out his tool and began cutting through his arm. After an excruciatingly painful hour, he was finally free.

The stump wrapped in a plastic grocery bag, Ralston placed it in a sling fashioned from a water bottle. He then left his rock prison for the first time in five days. He told himself over and over, "no stupid mistakes." After carefully rappelling down the six-story-high Big Drop with one good arm, he found a puddle of the most "wonderfully sweet" water he had ever tasted.[14]

FINDING HELP

Finally in the sunlight, Ralston began walking the eight-mile (13 km) trek back to his truck, hoping he would not bleed

▲ In the film *127 Hours*, actor James Franco portrayed Ralston.

out before reaching it. At about mile six, he saw three figures ahead of him on the trail. He tried several times to call out, but his mouth was too parched to make a sound. At last, he heard himself yelling, "HELP!"[15]

The three people—a Dutch couple vacationing with their son—ran to him, shocked by the filthy bearded man with his arm drenched in blood. "I'm Aron," Ralston said. "I had to cut off my hand four hours ago. I've been stuck since Saturday. I need medical attention, and I need a helicopter."[16]

With the couple too stunned to act, Ralston took charge. He asked if they had food and water. He gobbled down the two cookies and guzzled the water they gave him. He then told the woman and her son to run ahead to the trailhead, where they said authorities were already looking for him.

The Dutch man and another hiker they encountered continued on with Ralston, who doubted

STAYING HYDRATED

After emerging from Bluejohn Canyon, Ralston began an eight-mile (13 km) hike to the trailhead. After just one mile (1.6 km), he had only 1.1 quart (1 L) of water left. He knew he had to figure out a way to preserve his precious water supply.[17] Ralston suddenly remembered reading a running magazine article about the Rarámuri (Tarahumara) people of Mexico. Running long distances in the desert, they hold a few sips of water in their mouths, which humidifies the air in their lungs. The trick worked for Ralston. He was able to press on without drinking all his water.

⚠ Helicopters play an important role in search and rescue operations. They can bring rescuers into a wilderness area, reducing the time it takes to reach a person in need of help.

he could survive walking much farther. Suddenly, the three men heard a whirring overhead. They waved their hands in the air, attracting the attention of a helicopter pilot. The helicopter landed, and Ralston was taken aboard and flown to a hospital. He later found out that his mother realized he was missing and asked for the help of his climbing friends. Through their efforts, Ralston's truck was spotted at the Horseshoe Canyon trailhead, prompting the arrival of the rescue helicopter. If the helicopter had not already been in the area, Ralston would have likely died before receiving medical help.

A LIFE-CHANGING SELF-RESCUE

Ralston's rescue became international news. Over months of rehabilitation, he received letters from around the globe from admirers who saw him as a role model of resilience and survival. Emerging as a celebrity in the world of adventure sports, he told his story in motivational speeches at companies, organizations, and schools. He also wrote about his experiences in Bluejohn Canyon in his best-selling book *Between a Rock and a Hard Place*. It was made into the 2010 Academy Award–nominated film *127 Hours*.

When speaking about his ordeal, Ralston always expresses gratitude for how the experience taught him about the most important things in life. To remember this lesson, he has returned many times to Bluejohn Canyon. During each visit, he makes a point of feeling the boulder's surface with the fingers of his remaining hand. As he has explained, "I touch it and go back to that place, remembering . . . this quest to want to get out of there and return to love and relationships."[18]

CULTURAL IMPACT
127 HOURS

In late 2010, film festivals began to screen *127 Hours,* a movie directed by Danny Boyle based on Ralston's book *Between a Rock and a Hard Place*. The news was filled with stories of viewers fainting in theaters when they watched the scene in which Ralston, played by James Franco, cut off his own arm to free himself from the boulder.

The movie ended up resonating with both audiences and critics, but not just because of the response to that single scene. Keeping the camera tight on the Ralston character, Boyle wanted the audience to so identify with him that, when he freed himself, "they'd get released as well."[19] *New York Times* critic A. O. Scott hailed the movie as a "perversely inspirational story" that "leaves you with the impression of having lived, vicariously but intensely, through something whose meaning is both profound and elusive."[20] A hit at the box office, *127 Hours* was nominated for six Academy Awards, including Best Picture.

▲ Ralston attended the premier of *127 Hours* at New York's Chelsea Clearview Cinema in 2010.

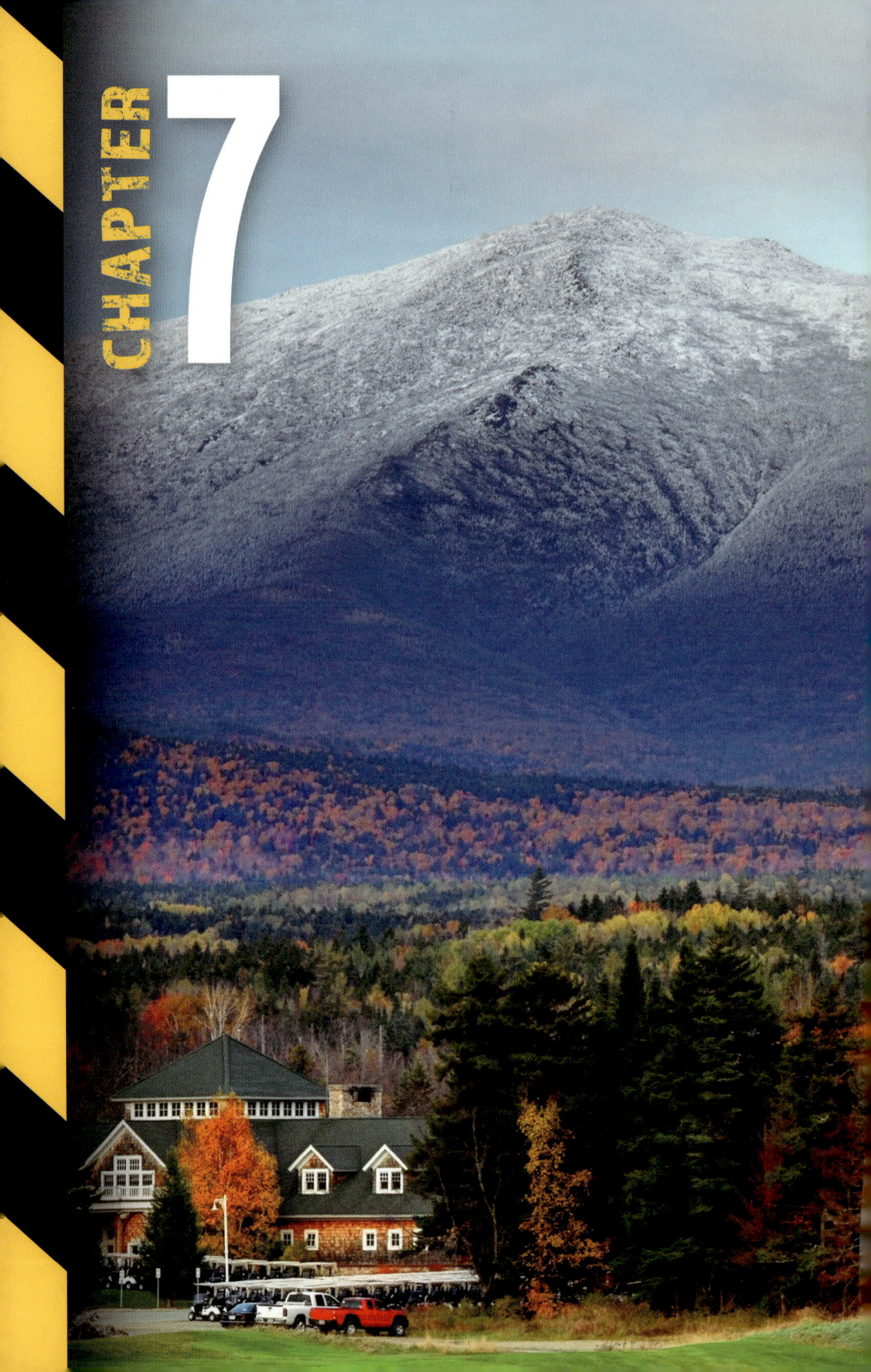

CHAPTER 7

SAVING JOHN

In the early morning of October 17, 2010, Pam Bales was eagerly checking the forecast. She was hoping weather conditions were mild enough that she could take a late-season hike to the summit of Mount Washington, the highest peak in the White Mountains of New Hampshire. The forecast predicted some wind and low clouds, but Bales decided the conditions were safe enough to try a six-hour hike on a trail loop that would take her from the trailhead to the summit and back.

Bales had reason to be confident. A nurse and a mountain guide, she had grown up in New Hampshire and had hiked the trail by herself countless times. For the last five years, she had also been a member of the

◀ The Abenaki name for Mount Washington is Agiocochook.

Pemigewasset Valley Search and Rescue Team. Working with the team, she was well trained for any safety issues she might face while on a climb.

A CHANGE IN THE WEATHER

Before setting out, Bales left a copy of her itinerary on her car dashboard. She had also given copies to two friends on the rescue team. In preparation for her adventure, she loaded her backpack with plenty of supplies. She included clothing so she could put on more layers as she neared the chilly mountaintop.

When Bales set out on the snow-covered Jewell Trail, the sun was bright. She wore a fleece tank top so she could feel its warmth on her bare arms. But early in her ascent, she quickly sensed the weather was changing. By nine o'clock that morning, she had put on a fleece top and gloves. By 10:30 a.m., she had added a jacket, mountaineering mittens, and goggles.

Bales saw thick clouds dropping below the mountain's peak. As she crossed the tree line and neared the junction of Jewell Trail and Gulfside Trail, she felt the temperature drop dramatically. Bales was experienced enough to realize she had to make a change of plans. This was not the day to climb to the summit. In fact, she needed to get back to the trailhead as quickly as she could.

A TRAIL OF FOOTPRINTS

As heavy sleet began to rain down on her, Bales spied something frightening—a series of footprints heading off the path. No hiker should have been walking off the trail in such harsh weather conditions. But even worse, the footprints were made by sneakers, which were completely inadequate for mountain climbing in the snow.

During her rescue training, it had been drilled into Bales that she should never put her own life at risk when trying to rescue a hiker in danger. She knew the safest thing for her to do was to return to the trailhead immediately. But instead, she stopped and yelled, "Hello!" in the direction of

THE DANGEROUS MOUNT WASHINGTON

Mount Washington is a popular destination for hikers and climbers. But the 6,288-foot (1,917 m) mountain has a very high fatality record.[1] Since 1849, more than 160 people have died on Mount Washington.[2] The mountain, especially in the winter, is said to have some of the worst weather in the world. Ice on the trails, extremely low temperatures, and hurricane-force winds are just a few of the adverse conditions mountaineers often face on their way to its summit.

▲ The weather and temperature can change quickly in the mountains. It's important that people venturing into the mountains be prepared.

the footprints. There was no response. She called out, "Is anybody there? Do you need help?"[3] Again, all she heard was the wind.

In case the endangered hiker could not hear her voice, she blew her rescue whistle. Bales then walked a few feet along the path of footprints and spied a man sitting in the snow with his back against a boulder. She was shocked to see that all he was wearing was a light jacket and a pair of shorts. Bales walked toward him, saying, "Oh, hello," but he ignored her. "He was breathing, but his skin looked like porcelain and he wore a vacant expression," she later recalled.[4] It was then Bales realized that her afternoon hike had turned into a rescue mission.

TO THE RESCUE

Bales asked the man his name. The man said nothing. Because of her medical training, she recognized from his pale skin and glazed expression that he was in danger of dying from hypothermia. To save him, the first thing she had to do was get him out of his soaking wet clothing. She stripped him down to his T-shirt and underwear and examined him but found no injuries. Bales then dressed him in winter clothing from her own pack. Now that he was her patient, she felt a need to address him by a name. Bales started calling the silent man John.

Bales fished a thermos of hot chocolate out of her backpack and dropped a few electrolyte cubes inside. These cubes are used to restore the balance of important minerals in the body, particularly potassium, that can be thrown off by hypothermia. She pulled back John's head and poured the warm liquid down his throat. For the first time, John began to speak to her, though his speech was still slurred. He explained that he had driven from Maine that morning to hike the trail loop but had gotten lost.

It had taken a full hour to dress John. Bales knew they had to leave immediately if they were to reach the trailhead before dark. Looking him directly in the eyes, she said, "John, we have to go now!"[5] Bales told him she would lead and he would follow. She cautioned him sternly to stay right behind her. She did not like using aggressive language, but she knew she had to get through to John if both of them were going to survive.

IN IT TOGETHER

The first stretch along Gulfside Trail was slow going. The wind had wiped away Bales's own footprints, so she had to follow the path by looking for the small holes her hiking poles had left in the snow. To focus her mind and to keep John conscious, she began to sing Elvis Presley songs. Occasionally she would ask John a question, but he answered only in grunts.

At one point, John sat in the snow, curling his body into a ball with his hands on his knees. Bales realized he was giving up. "That's not an option, John," she said.[6] After she

> ### A FAILED RESCUE
>
> Ty Gagne, who brought popular attention to Bales's rescue of John, has written about another White Mountains rescue effort. In the book *Where You'll Find Me*, he recounts how Kate Matrosova, a 32-year-old experienced climber, set off to climb Mount Madison on February 15, 2015. Within hours, an unexpected cold front blew in. Matrosova activated a personal location beacon, alerting the authorities that she was in trouble. Rescuers set out but could not find her in the blizzard conditions. The next morning, Matrosova's body was discovered. She had died of exposure after being blown off the trail by hurricane-force winds.

reminded him, "We're in this together," he got up and began following her again.⁷

They finally reached the Jewell Trail, where the downward hike became easier. After they passed the tree line, trees once again protected them from the bitter wind. Bales kept singing and encouraging John, but she was terrified he might drop down into the snow again and give up for good.

A LIFE SAVED

Six hours after Bales had found John, they stumbled into the dark parking lot at the trailhead. She started her car and used its heater to dry his wet clothes. Now that they were safe, Bales began grilling John. "Why didn't you check the weather forecast dressed like that?" she asked.⁸ He said nothing. He put on his dry clothes, thanked her, and drove off in his car. She stood in the parking lot, confused. Over the next few days, she became angry at John. She kept thinking how ungrateful he was.

About a week later, a letter with a small donation arrived at the office of her rescue group. The writer said he was the man Bales had called John, but he declined to reveal his real name. He explained that he had hoped to die

> "The entire time [Pam Bales] treated me with care, compassion, authority, confidence and the impression that I mattered. With all that has been going wrong in my life, I didn't matter to me, but I did to Pam. . . . Maybe I wasn't meant to die yet, I somehow still mattered in life.[9]"
>
> —From John's letter to the Pemigewasset Valley Search and Rescue Team

on the trail that day. He had purposely dressed the way he did so death would come quickly. As Bales led him down the mountain, he kept thinking of running away. But he was afraid she would chase after him, and he did not want her to die. The understanding and care she showed him made him reconsider his plan to kill himself. The man explained that he was now in therapy for his mental illness and was getting help with finding a job. At the end of the note, he thanked Bales for everything she had done for him.

INFINITE STORM

The story of Bales's rescue of John became a legend among White Mountain hikers. But it was largely unknown outside that community until writer Ty Gagne told the tale in a long article in *Appalachia Journal* in 2018. The next year, Gagne's story was reprinted on the website of the *New Hampshire*

⚠ Search and rescue volunteers must carry all the essential gear for their mission. They also receive wilderness survival training.

Union Leader. It became one of the most popular stories ever published on that newspaper's site.

Among its many readers was actor and aspiring screenwriter Joshua Rollins. Having hiked the White Mountains many times, he was fascinated by Bales's story and was convinced it could make a great movie. Gagne's article and Rollins's interviews with Bales became the basis for his screenplay for the 2022 film *Infinite Storm*, in which actress Naomi Watts played Bales. Throughout the filming, Bales was in contact with Rollins and Watts to

▲ Pam Bales, *right*, attended a screening of Infinite Storm in 2022. Naomi Watts, *left*, played Bales.

answer their questions so the movie would be as accurate as possible.

Still, the filmmakers took some liberties with Bales's story. One was the location. The movie was filmed in the Alps in Slovenia rather than the White Mountains. Her hiking friends noticed. The film also ends with a meeting between Bales and John after they survived their ordeal on Mount Washington. In real life, though, they did not see each other afterward. Even without knowing what happened with John, Bales remains convinced, based on their time together, that he is a survivor. As she has explained, "I like to think he is out there somewhere, enjoying his second chance."[10]

BEING PREPARED

Aside from enjoying the inspirational story, Bales hopes audiences who see *Infinite Storm* take from it an important message: always be well prepared before going on a hike. While working on the rescue team on Mount Washington, she most frequently had to help people who had hiked a trail as a spur-of-the-moment decision. As she told a reporter in 2022, "They say let's go on a hike, with flip flops and a 12-ounce [350 mL] bottle of water . . . thinking 'I will conquer the mountain,' and that gets them in trouble most every time."[11]

CHAPTER 8

SURVIVING ROCKS AND MOUNTAINS

Before ascending the Ogre, Doug Scott had assembled a team he could trust, and they came to his aid when disaster struck. Even though she was going on a day hike, Pam Bales packed all the supplies she needed to save not only herself but also a distressed stranger when the weather unexpectedly turned. Alone and terrified, Aron Ralston had enough climbing knowledge and experience to assess his options and choose the only course he knew that could save his life. These stories show that surviving in rocky and mountainous terrains is not just a matter of luck. Preparation, experience, and education also

◀ Being prepared is important for staying safe on any mountain or canyon adventure.

PREVENTING HEAD INJURIES

Until recently, many rock and mountain climbers did not wear helmets. Existing helmets were large and uncomfortable. They offered some protection from falling rocks but did not help much when climbers fell and knocked their heads. Newer helmets, designed to be lightweight and well ventilated, are becoming more popular. They are particularly beneficial to rock climbers, who with a single misstep are in danger of finding themselves hanging upside down from their ropes with their head swinging dangerously close to a rock face.

play a large role in turning potential tragedy into an inspiring tale of survival.

For anyone wanting to explore rocky areas, climbing skills are essential. Taking climbing classes or being trained by an experienced climber provides an introduction to the necessary gear, such as harnesses, ropes, and anchors, and how to use it safely. Becoming part of a climbing community also makes it easier for beginners to find a team of trained climbers to join on outings.

Other essential gear includes helmets and climbing shoes or boots. Well-fitting boots are especially important for mountain trails because tight boots can interfere with blood circulation, making the feet feel colder. Crampons, metal spikes that attach to footwear, might be needed to hike or climb in areas with ice and snow. When there is snow on the ground, sunglasses or goggles also are needed to prevent snow blindness.

Clothing choices should be determined by the weather and the environment. If rain or snow is expected, wearing a moisture-wicking layer as a base will keep the skin dry. When heading into cold, mountainous areas, it is best to bring additional clothing so layers can be added as temperatures drop nearer the summit or as weather conditions change. In hot and dry environments, T-shirts and shorts may appear the natural choice. But to avoid sunburn, lightweight clothes that cover more skin can be a better option.

BACKPACK TIPS

A well-stocked backpack can be the best preparation for any unexpected situations on the trail. For most outings, essential items include extra clothing, a first aid kit, matches or a lighter, and a knife or multi-tool. Sunscreen and sunglasses are also important. An emergency blanket can be helpful in a cold environment. Even on short trips, a headlight or flashlight is a must because unexpected delays might push the end of the hike or climb to after sunset.

The most important thing to pack is adequate food and water. Foods like nuts, granola, dried fruit, and jerky are good for most day trips because they store well and do not need to be cooked. As a guideline, a climber or hiker

▲ Backpacks are better for long outings than shoulder packs because they spread weight more evenly across the body.

should pack three quarts (2.8 L) of water for each day.[1] But more might be needed when traveling in hot weather, in dry environments, or at high altitudes.

Planning the route is crucial. The route needs to match the skill level of everyone taking it. To avoid veering off course, it is smart to pack a cell phone equipped with GPS and to bring a map and compass as a backup. An itinerary for the trip should always be left with an emergency contact. Checking the weather should be the last step before heading out to make sure there have been no unexpected changes in the forecast.

PAYING ATTENTION

Having an outdoor adventure should be fun. But to stay safe, people among rocks or in the mountains need to concentrate on each step, being careful not to walk or climb too fast or to place their feet on wet or icy patches. Everyone in a group should talk as little as possible. Too much conversation can distract climbers and lead to accidents.

Climbers also must pay attention to changing conditions. If the weather turns unexpectedly stormy or cold, it is best to turn back. Everyone should also keep tabs on how the others in their group are doing. If someone is overly fatigued and cannot keep up, the party should turn back and plan the outing for another day.

KEEPING QUIET

Lynn Hill is a legendary rock climber. But she made a serious mistake while climbing in France in 1989. Distracted by a conversation she was having, Hill did not fully tie a knot in a rope attached to her harness. As a result, Hill fell 75 feet (23 m) before hitting the ground. Hill survived, but her error is a cautionary tale for climbers at all skill levels.[2] To avoid injury, rock and mountain climbers always need to stay focused on the task at hand.

Rock and mountain climbers should also look out for falling rocks. They need to listen carefully as well. A rumbling sound can signal that a rockfall is about to happen. When resting, people should not sit directly below a vertical

> **Your performance on the mountain you climbed last week or last month or last year doesn't matter—because it's all about what you are doing right now.**[3]
>
> —Alison Levine, mountaineer and author of On the Edge

cliff, or else they might be in the path of falling debris.

While in rocky terrain, adventurers should stay hydrated by taking sips of water before they become thirsty. In hot and dry areas, they should be aware if they start experiencing headaches, dizziness, sweating, and other signs of heatstroke. Anyone experiencing those symptoms should seek out shade, drink plenty of water, and apply water-soaked cloths to their armpits and neck.

People on cold mountains also need to constantly monitor how they are feeling. Climbers with headaches or nausea should stop their ascent because they could be suffering from altitude sickness. If they have a splitting headache or wet cough, they are at risk of a severe case and should descend as soon as possible.

It is also important to look out for signs of frostbite and hypothermia, which often appear together. The pain of mild frostbite can be relieved by warming the hands in the armpits or by placing the feet against the body of another team member. Anyone showing signs of hypothermia, such as drowsiness or shivering, should first be moved out of the cold. They then need to be stripped of any wet clothing and given dry, warm clothes or wrapped in blankets. Drinking warm beverages can also help restore a normal body temperature.

If someone suffers severe illness or injury in rocky terrain, it is crucial to get the victim medical attention quickly. Self-rescue is best if the climbing team can help the victim themselves. But if that is impossible, they must be prepared to call 911 for a rescue team.

With all the planning and effort that goes into safely navigating rocky and mountainous terrain, it is natural to wonder if it is worth it. But veteran climbers have no doubt that it is. For many, the rewards of overcoming physical challenges to experience some of the world's most thrilling landscapes are far greater than the risks involved.

EMERGENCY BEACONS

Cell phone service on high mountains and in remote rocky locations is spotty at best. Climbers in peril have another way to signal for help. They can activate a device called an emergency beacon. Using satellite technology, the beacon sends its location to a global monitoring center in Texas. The center then contacts authorities near the location of the climber in need of rescue.

ESSENTIAL FACTS

SURVIVAL STORIES

- In 1972, survivors of a plane crash in the Andes Mountains of Chile stayed alive by eating the bodies of those who had died. After rescue teams gave up their search, two young men in the group volunteered to journey over a mountain and summon help, ending the survivors' 71-day ordeal.

- While descending the Ogre, a great rock tower in Pakistan, in 1977, British mountaineer Doug Scott broke both of his legs when his body slammed against a rock face. Only through Scott's determination and the teamwork of his five climbing partners was he able to return to the safety of base camp.

- During an ill-fated climb in the Peruvian Andes in 1985, Simon Yates had to cut the rope connecting him to his climbing partner Joe Simpson, plunging Simpson into a deep crevasse. With a broken leg, Simpson managed to escape the crevasse and descend the mountain.

- On a solo climbing adventure in Utah in 2003, Aron Ralston was trapped in a narrow, isolated canyon when his forearm and hand were pinned to a rock wall by a boulder. He amputated his own arm to survive.

- Caught in a winter storm in 2010 while hiking New Hampshire's Mount Washington, mountain rescuer Pam Bales encountered a suicidal stranger suffering from hypothermia. Risking her own life, Bales used her climbing know-how and encouraging words to guide the man she called John safely off the mountain.

ROCK AND MOUNTAIN SURVIVAL

- Mountains are landforms that reach a high elevation, have sleep slopes, and have a small area at their summit.

- Rocky areas include canyons and mesas. Canyons are deep valleys with steep sides. Mesas are flat-topped hills with steep sides.

- People on cold mountains should watch out for signs of frostbite, hypothermia, dehydration, and altitude sickness.

- People venturing into hot, dry, rocky areas should monitor themselves for heat exhaustion, heatstroke, and dehydration.

- Avalanches and rockfalls are common dangers in mountainous and rocky terrain.

- Precautions include planning a route, packing the proper supplies and gear, leaving an itinerary with a trusted friend, checking the weather, and carrying a mobile phone or other communication device to call for help if disaster strikes.

QUOTE

"Climb if you will, but remember that courage and strength are nought without prudence, and that a momentary negligence may destroy the happiness of a life."

—*Edward Whymper, who became the first person to climb the Matterhorn in 1865*

GLOSSARY

acclimate
To adjust to a new climate or environment.

altitude
The height of an object in relation to sea level.

clairvoyant
Someone who is said to be able to perceive things not apparent to the physical senses.

climate
The average weather in a region over a period of years.

crevasse
A deep open crack, usually in a glacier.

erosion
The process by which rock is worn away by water, wind, and other natural forces.

extremity
A limb of the body.

frostbite
Damage to bodily tissue—particularly in the fingers, toes, and nose—due to exposure to extreme cold.

fuselage
The body of an airplane.

itinerary
The planned route of a trip; a planned list of stops on a trip.

plateau
An area of level ground that is higher than the surrounding area.

rappel
To lower oneself down a mountain or rock face using a harness and climbing rope.

rockfall
The falling of loose rocks and rocky debris from a cliff or a mountainside.

snow blindness
A medical condition caused by damage to the eye by lengthy exposure to ultraviolet rays reflected off snow and ice.

summit
The top of a volcano or mountain.

taboo
Forbidden due to moral, social, or religious customs.

terrain
An area of land with distinct physical features.

tourniquet
A device, such as a piece of cloth, that is wrapped tightly around a leg or an arm to prevent blood loss from a wound.

tree line
The altitude above which trees can no longer grow.

ADDITIONAL RESOURCES

SELECTED BIBLIOGRAPHY

Ralston, Aron. *Between a Rock and a Hard Place*. Kindle ed., Atria, 2004.

Read, Piers Paul. *Alive: The Story of the Andes Survivors*. Pan, 1974. *Internet Archive*, archive.org. Accessed 6 July 2023.

Scott, Doug. *The Ogre*. Kindle ed., Vertebrate, 2017.

Simpson, Joe. *Touching the Void*. Kindle ed., Directauthors.com, 1988.

FURTHER READINGS

Olson, Tod. *Into the Clouds: The Race to Climb the World's Most Dangerous Mountain*. Scholastic Focus, 2020.

Towell, Colin. *The Survival Handbook: Essential Skills for Outdoor Adventure*. DK, 2020.

Wheeler, Jill C. *Extreme Cold Survival Stories*. Abdo, 2024.

ONLINE RESOURCES

To learn more about rocky and mountainous areas and survival, please visit **abdobooklinks.com** or scan this QR code. These links are routinely monitored and updated to provide the most current information available.

MORE INFORMATION

For more information on this subject, contact or visit the following organizations:

AMERICAN ALPINE CLUB
710 10th St., Ste. 100
Golden, CO 80401
info@americanalpineclub.org
americanalpineclub.org

The American Alpine Club is an organization that promotes all types of climbing, whether on mountains, on rock faces, or in the gym. It organizes climbing festivals and provides grants to help preserve endangered climbing areas.

THE MOUNTAINEERS
7700 Sand Point Way NE
Seattle, WA 98115
info@mountaineers.org
mountaineers.org

The Mountaineers hosts climbs and hikes, provides lessons on climbing, and operates a publishing company specializing in climbing and mountaineering.

YOSEMITE CLIMBING MUSEUM AND GALLERY
5180 Hwy. 140
Mariposa, CA 95338
yosemiteclimbing.org/museuminfo

Operated by the Yosemite Climbing Association, the museum preserves the history of climbing throughout the world with displays of historic photographs, climbing gear, and other climbing-related memorabilia.

SOURCE NOTES

CHAPTER 1. STRANDED IN THE ANDES

1. James Vlahos. "Then Alive! And Now." *National Geographic Adventure*, Apr. 2006. 46.

2. *Stranded*. Directed by Gonzalo Arijón, Zeitgeist Films, 2008.

3. Amy Tikkanen. "Uruguayan Air Force Flight 571." *Encyclopedia Britannica*, 5 Jan. 2023, britannica.com. Accessed 6 July 2023.

4. Vlahos, "Then Alive!"

5. *Stranded*.

6. *Stranded*.

7. Chris Skudder. "Alive: Rugby Team's Fabled Survival in Andes." *Sky News*, 10 Oct. 2015, news.sky.com. Accessed 6 July 2023.

8. *Stranded*.

9. Don Podesta. "Echoes of a Crash Unheard Of." *Washington Post*, 21 Dec. 1992, washingtonpost.com. Accessed 6 July 2023.

10. Piers Paul Read. *Alive: The Story of the Andes Survivors*. Pan, 1974. 69. *Internet Archive*, archive.org. Accessed 6 July 2023.

11. Read, *Alive*, 69.

CHAPTER 2. THE DANGERS OF ROCKS AND MOUNTAINS

1. "About Grand Canyon Animals." *Grand Canyon Visitor Center*, n.d., explorethecanyon.com. Accessed 6 July 2023.

2. Edward Whymper. *Scrambles amongst the Alps*. John Murray, 1936. 334. *Internet Archive*, archive.org. Accessed 6 July 2023.

3. "Essential Skills: Coping with Heat." *Mountaineering Scotland*, n.d., mountaineering.scot. Accessed 6 July 2023.

4. Virginia Van Vynckt. "Why Do You Need to Drink a Lot of Water at a High Altitude?" *Livestrong.com*, n.d., livestrong.com. Accessed 6 July 2023.

5. "Avalanche Safety: How to Avoid Getting Buried." *American Alpine Institute*, Dec. 2005, alpineinstitute.com. Accessed 6 July 2023.

6. Matthew Haag and Matt Stevens. "Second Yosemite Rockfall in Two Days Injures One at El Capitan." *New York Times*, 28 Sept. 2018, nytimes.com. Accessed 6 July 2023.

7. Simon Rauch, Bernd Wallner, Mathias Ströhle, Tomas Dal Cappello and Monika Brodmann Maeder. "Climbing Accidents—Prospective Data Analysis from the International Alpine Trauma Registry and Systematic Review of the Literature." *International Journal of Environmental Research and Public Health*, vol. 17, no. 1, 27 Dec. 2019, ncbi.nlm.nih.gov. Accessed 18 July 2023.

CHAPTER 3. OVER THE MOUNTAIN

1. James Vlahos. "Then Alive! And Now." *National Geographic Adventure*, Apr. 2006. 46.

2. Piers Paul Read. *Alive: The Story of the Andes Survivors*. Pan, 1974. 193. *Internet Archive*, archive.org. Accessed 6 July 2023.

3. Don Podesta. "Echoes of a Crash Unheard Of." *Washington Post*, 21 Dec. 1992, washingtonpost.com. Accessed 6 July 2023.

INDEX

altitude sickness, 22–23, 45, 98
Anthoine, Julian "Mo", 40, 42, 44–48, 50

backpacks, 69, 82, 85, 95
Bales, Pam, 81–91, 93
beacons, 86, 99
Between a Rock and a Hard Place, 78, 79
Bonington, Chris, 39–42, 44–50
Braithwaite, Paul "Tut," 40, 46–47

Canessa, Roberto, 8–9, 30–35, 37
canyons, 15, 18–20, 67, 77
    Bluejohn Canyon, 69–71, 72, 76, 78
    Grand Canyon, 15, 18–19
Chile, 5, 7, 12, 13, 27, 30–31, 36
climate change, 25
clothing, 31–32, 54, 55, 61, 82, 85, 87, 95, 98–99
crevasses, 57–60

dehydration, 23, 61

Estcourt, Nick, 40, 46–48

frostbite, 21, 48, 98

Gagne, Ty, 86, 88–89

Hawking, Richard, 54, 59, 61, 63
heat exhaustion, 21
heatstroke, 21, 98
helicopters, 36, 48–50, 55, 71, 76–77
helmets, 94
Hill, Lynn, 97
hypothermia, 20–21, 85, 98

Infinite Storm, 89, 91
injuries, 8–9, 20, 24–25, 34, 40, 42, 44, 49, 64, 85, 94, 99

Maspons, Daniel, 27–28
Matrosova, Kate, 86
mountains, 13, 15–18, 20, 22–24, 25, 39, 42, 47, 50, 53, 64, 67–68, 81, 86, 89, 91, 93–95, 97–99
    Alps, 16, 21, 53, 91
    Andes Mountains, 6, 7, 9, 10, 12, 16, 27–33, 34, 36–37, 53
    Baintha Brakk (the Ogre), 39–43, 47–50, 93
    Everest, Mount, 15, 40, 64
    Himalayas, 16–18
    Rocky Mountains, 16
    Siula Grande, 53–58, 63
    Washington, Mount, 81–82, 83, 88, 91

CHAPTER 7. SAVING JOHN

1. Alison Osius. "The New Movie 'Infinite Storm' Chronicles a One-Woman Mountain Rescue." *Outside*, 5 Apr. 2022, climbing.com. Accessed 6 July 2023.

2. Jackson Cote. "While Hiking Mt. Washington in New Hampshire with His Son, 46-Year-Old Man Collapses and Dies." *MassLive Media*, 27 Aug. 2022, masslive.com. Accessed 6 July 2023.

3. Ty Gagne. "Emotional Rescue." *Be Outdoors Appalachian Mountain Club*, 17 Jan. 2019, outdoors.org. Accessed 6 July 2023.

4. Pam Bales. "Mountain Mystery." *Backpacker*. Nov./Dec. 2020. 40–41.

5. Gagne, "Emotional Rescue."

6. Gagne, "Emotional Rescue."

7. Bales, "Mountain Mystery."

8. Gagne, "Emotional Rescue."

9. Gagne, "Emotional Rescue."

10. Bales, "Mountain Mystery."

11. David Brooks. "Story of Mount Washington Rescue Makes It to the Big Screen, but the Mountain Does Not." *Concord Monitor*, 11 Mar. 2022, concordmonitor.com. Accessed 6 July 2023.

CHAPTER 8. SURVIVING ROCKS AND MOUNTAINS

1. Laura Snider. "50 Common Climbing Mistakes." *Outside*, 24 Feb. 2022, climbing.com. Accessed 6 July 2023.

2. Snider, "50 Common Climbing Mistakes."

3. Alison Levine. *On the Edge: The Art of High-Impact Leadership*. Business Plus, 2014. 231.

SOURCE NOTES CONTINUED

CHAPTER 6. TRAPPED BY A BOULDER

1. Laurence Gonzales. "One Way Out." *National Geographic Adventure*, Aug. 2003. 38.

2. Gonzales, "One Way Out."

3. Aron Ralston. "Trapped: The Real Story of Aron Ralston." *MyMedic*, 25 July 2016, mymedic.com. Accessed 6 July 2023.

4. Gonzales, "One Way Out."

5. Ralston, "Trapped."

6. Ralston, "Trapped."

7. Gonzales, "One Way Out."

8. Devin Friedman. "Men of the Year: Survivor." *GQ*, 23 Nov. 2003, gq.com. Accessed 6 July 2023.

9. Ralston, "Trapped."

10. Ralston, "Trapped."

11. Friedman, "Men of the Year."

12. Ralston, "Trapped."

13. Ralston, "Trapped."

14. Aron Ralston. *Between a Rock and a Hard Place*. Kindle ed., Atria, 2004. 305.

15. Ralston, *Between a Rock and a Hard Place*, 311.

16. Gonzales, "One Way Out."

17. Ralston, *Between a Rock and a Hard Place*, 208–209.

18. Patrick Barkham. "The Extraordinary Story behind Danny Boyle's *127 Hours*." *Guardian*, 15 Dec. 2010, theguardian.com. Accessed 6 July 2023.

19. "Behind the Scenes of '127 Hours.'" *Hollywood Reporter*, n.d., hollywoodreporter.com. Accessed 6 July 2023.

20. A. O. Scott. "The Tale of a Shocking Fall and a Gritty Resolve." *New York Times*, 4 Nov. 2010, nytimes.com. Accessed 6 July 2023.

4. Read, *Alive*, 305.

5. *Stranded*. Directed by Gonzalo Arijón, Zeitgeist Films, 2008.

CHAPTER 4. DESCENDING THE OGRE

1. Doug Scott. *The Ogre*. Kindle ed., Vertebrate, 2017. 10.

2. Scott, *The Ogre*, 94.

3. Christian Bonington. "The Ogre." *American Alpine Club*, 1978, publications.americanalpineclub.org. Accessed 6 July 2023.

4. Scott, *The Ogre*, 95.

5. Scott, *The Ogre*, 94.

6. Scott, *The Ogre*, 98.

7. Bonington, "The Ogre."

8. Scott, *The Ogre*, 100.

9. Scott, *The Ogre*, 109.

10. Scott, *The Ogre*, 103.

11. Scott, *The Ogre*, 106.

12. Scott, *The Ogre*, 105.

13. Scott, *The Ogre*, 108.

14. "Sir Chris Bonington Climbs the Old Man of Hoy Again after 48 Years." *BBC News*, 20 Aug. 2014, bbc.com. Accessed 6 July 2023.

15. "Sir Chris Bonington Climbs the Old Man of Hoy for 80th Birthday." *PlanetMountain.com*, 1 Sept. 2014, planetmountain.com. Accessed 6 July 2023.

16. Bonington, "The Ogre."

17. Bonington, "The Ogre."

CHAPTER 5. THE END OF THE ROPE

1. "Touching the Void." *Scripts*, n.d., scripts.com. Accessed 6 July 2023.

2. "Touching the Void."

3. "Touching the Void."

4. "Touching the Void."

5. "Touching the Void."

6. "Touching the Void."

7. Rich Roberts. "Mountainside Miracle." *Los Angeles Times*, 28 Feb. 1989, latimes.com. Accessed 6 July 2023.

8. Roberts, "Mountainside Miracle."

9. "Touching the Void."

10. "Touching the Void."

11. Joe Simpson. *Touching the Void*. Kindle ed., Directauthors.com, 1988. Accessed 6 July 2023.

12. Tim Lewis. "Joe Simpson: To Be a Serious Climber, You Have to Be a Little Bit Unhinged." *Guardian*, 9 Nov. 2019, theguardian.com. Accessed 6 July 2023.

13. Lewis, "Joe Simpson."

14. Lewis, "Joe Simpson."

multi-tools, 71, 95

New Hampshire, 81, 88
Nicolich, Gustavo, 12

Old Man of Hoy, 49
127 Hours, 78, 79

Pakistan, 39, 47, 49
Parrado, Nando, 9, 12, 30–35, 37
Pemigewasset Valley Search and Rescue Team, 82, 88
Pérez, Marcelo, 9, 11–12, 29
Peru, 53–54, 64

rain shadows, 17
Ralston, Aron, 67–78, 79, 93
rappelling, 40–44, 46, 60, 69, 74
rivers, 18–19, 34, 69
Rowland, Clive, 40, 42, 44, 46–50

Scott, Doug, 39–44, 46–50, 93
Simpson, Joe, 53–54, 56–64

temperatures, 8, 17–18, 20–24, 25, 73, 82, 83, 95, 99
Touching the Void, 63–64
Turcatti, Numa, 27–28, 30, 32

Uruguay, 5–6, 7, 13, 27, 34, 36

Vizintín, Antonio, 30–33

water, 9, 23, 30, 34, 47, 55, 61, 69, 72, 74, 76, 91, 95–96, 98
weather, 20, 24, 30, 68, 81–83, 87, 93, 95–97
  flooding, 20, 25
  storms, 20, 43, 45–46, 57, 68, 97
  wind, 17, 20, 40, 43, 59, 81, 83, 84, 86–87

Yates, Simon, 53–59, 61, 63–64
Yosemite National Park, 24

Zerbino, Gustavo, 11, 27–28

ABOUT THE AUTHOR

LIZ SONNEBORN

A graduate of Swarthmore College, Liz Sonneborn has written more than 100 books for young readers and adults on a variety of subjects. Her specialties include American history, world history, biography, women's studies, and African American studies. Sonneborn has long lived in Brooklyn, New York, with her husband and two cats.